Superior Finger Exercises

Emanuel Ondrícek

edited by Charles Castleman
and Allyson Dawkins

B568

SOUTHERN MUSIC COMPANY

Emanuel Ondrícek was born in Pilsen (some biographies give his place of birth as Prague) on December 6, 1880, and he died in Boston on December 30, 1958. Emanuel Ondrícek was one of four violin playing sons of Jan Ondrícek. His older brother Franticek (Franz) was a protégé of Wieniawski who gave the premiere of the Dvorak Violin Concerto. The other brothers, Carl and Stanislav were also well-known. Like his brothers, Emanuel was a student of his father Jan. At fourteen, he entered the Conservatory at Prague where he was a student of Sevcik (1894-9), and of Ysaÿe (privately). He graduated with first prize five years later and was publicly congratulated for his splendid achievement by the president of the institution, Prince Ferdinand Lobkowitz, and the faculty. He toured throughout Europe, playing in Prague, Vienna, Budapest, Berlin, London, Petrograd and others, and performed as soloist under many famous conductors with such orchestras as the London Symphonic Orchestra, Queen's Hall Orchestra, the Berliner Philharmonie, Wiener Philharmonie, Prager Philharmonie, Russian Imperial Orchestra of Petrograd, and many others. He played for the Tsar and his Imperial Suite, also for the Rumanian Queen (Carmen Sylva) and the Serbian King and was decorated with the Russian and Serbian orders for his art. His debut tour of the United States was particularly successful.

Emanuel Ondrícek studied composition and counterpoint with Professors Knittl and Stecker and attended orchestra classes conducted by Antonin Dvorak. His compositions included several compositions for violin, several larger compositions for orchestra, a string quartet (1924) and popular arrangements of works by Fiorillo, Geminiani and Mondonville for violin and piano. He was a conductor of some success, described as "a conductor of decision and authority" *(Boston Herald)*. He was considered an authority on Slavic music.

From 1912 he devoted himself exclusively to teaching in Boston and New York City; in the late 1940s he was appointed Professor of Violin at Boston University. His students included Ruth Posselt, one of the first American woman violinists to make an international mark as a soloist.

* * * * *

I studied with Emanuel Ondrícek as a child from 1949 to 1956; he gave wise advice for career development in addition to instrumental instruction. His pedagogy is described in *The Mastery of Tone-Production and Expression on the Violin* (1931). His analytic practice system synthesized transcendent technical and musical mastery from accessible constituent kernels. His students were praised for their musical fervor and remarkable left-hand facility. His particular strength as a teacher of the right arm was a precisely planned bow distribution for enhanced phrasing and communication.

Charles Castleman

The text and images below were taken from promotional materials produced to accompany Ondrícek's first appearances in the United States.

Mr. Ondricek as he appeared after receiving his second decoration and shortly before he came to America.

Mr. Ondricek's teaching is referred to as the *"Grand School"* (*"Le Figaro,"* Paris, March 14th, 1924, after Miss Sinayeff's concert), while other papers rank Mr. Ondricek as a *"master"* (Huchard in *"Courier Musicale,"* Nov. 18th, 1925).

After Miss Pierce Posselt's phenomenal success in New York and Boston, the American critics also wrote laudatory comments on his teaching.

Mr. Ondricek is widely sought for coaching and preparing a repertoire for the concert stage, and in his "master class" are artist-pupils who *had previously studies with great teachers,* such as Ysaye, Auer, Cesar Thompson and Seveik.

Mr. Ondricek as he appeared while concertizing in Europe.

Introduction

The purpose of this book is to facilitate the learning of scales and arpeggios through a combination of visual and physical memory of the fingerboard. One must memorize scales and arpeggios to become fluent in the very rudiments of musical performance. Playing scales and arpeggios while seeing the notes with fingerings enables one to quickly learn and memorize by associating the sound of each pitch with the written note. In addition to scales and arpeggios, the finger patterns of Emanuel Ondrícek are an invaluable tool for playing repeated figures from memory and visualizing the fingerboard in all different keys. It may well be that the Ondrícek finger patterns contained in this book are appearing in print for the first time.

If you approach these exercises by learning the right place to put the fingers, then you will have a strong foundation for playing the violin accurately. Ultimately, careful listening is the way to play well in tune. In addition to listening, however, you can hone your intonation by visualizing the exact place on the fingerboard where each finger belongs, and the spaces between successive fingers. In stepwise motion, picture the distance of half steps or whole steps; in intervals, picture the distance of the space between the fingers. Let your ear guide your fingers, and learn the fingerboard by memorizing and visualizing. While each exercise is printed in a specific key, the exercises should be practiced in all keys, at a tempo of quarter note =72-104.

Some recommended points of focus are:

1. Practice in front of a mirror to be sure that your left hand position is good - wrist straight, and fingers close to the fingerboard.

2. Practice in front of a mirror to make certain that your bow is traveling parallel to the bridge.

3. While becoming increasingly aware of what the left hand does, also pay attention to the right hand. Knowing the levels of the fingerboard with the bow arm in coordination with the left hand is essential to mastery of technique; tactile memory is needed in both right and left hands.

Allyson Dawkins

This photograph was taken at Ondrícek's summer home in Cape Cod.
He and Charlie Castleman are playing Parchesi. It was 1948 and Charlie was 7.

SUPERIOR FINGER EXERCISES

B568

Emanuel Ondrícek
adapted by Allyson Dawkins

3

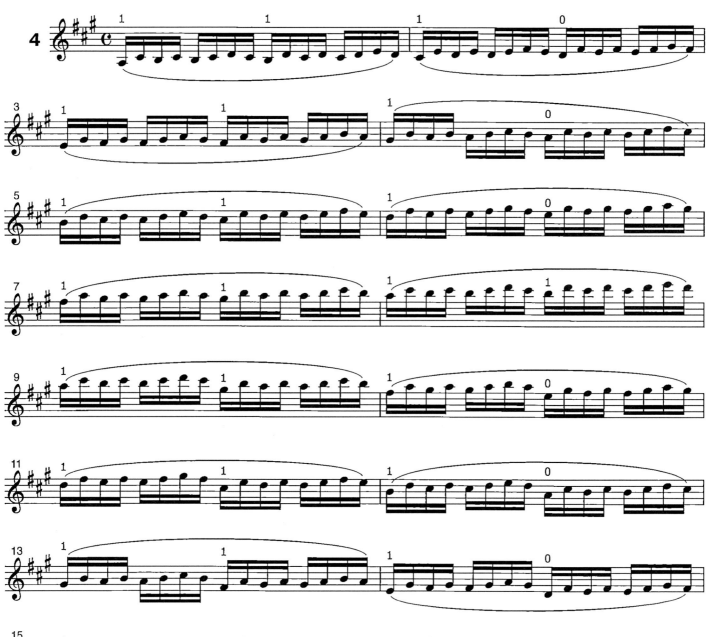

12

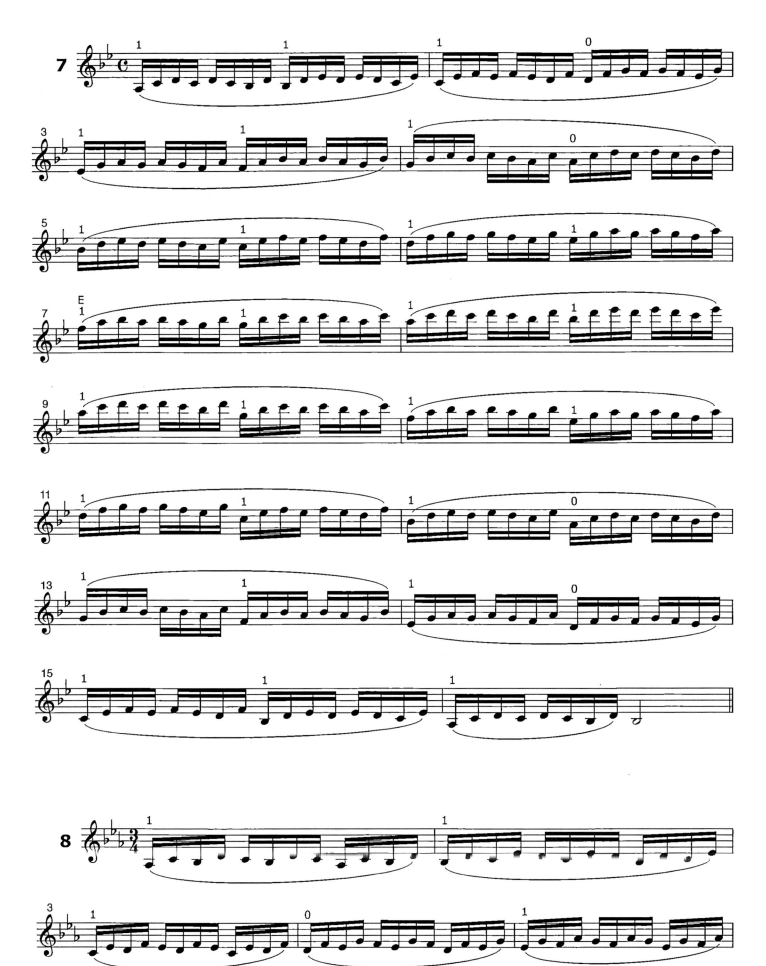

B568

CROSSING TWO STRINGS

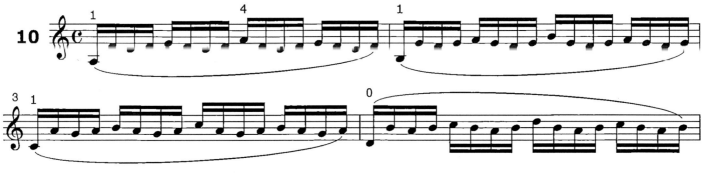

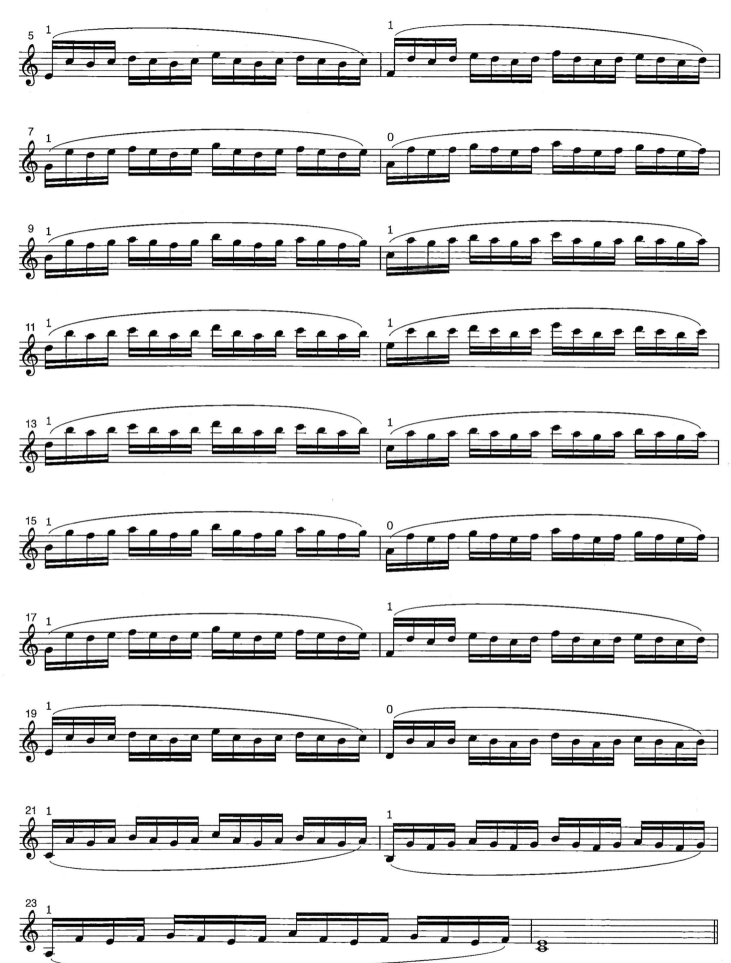

12

13

14

15

B568

22

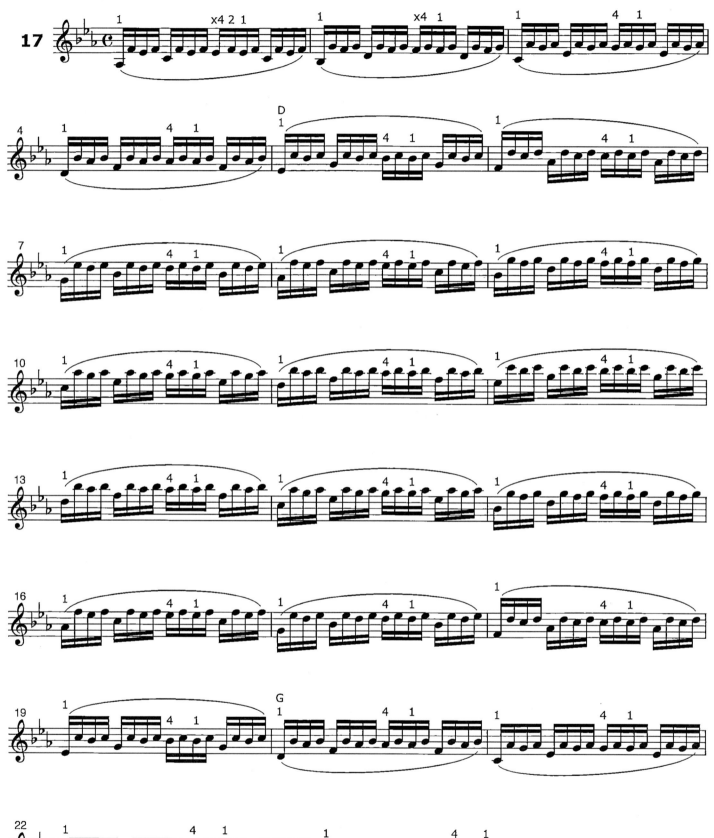

B568

CROSSING THREE STRINGS

22

23

25

26

27

CROSSING FOUR STRINGS

28

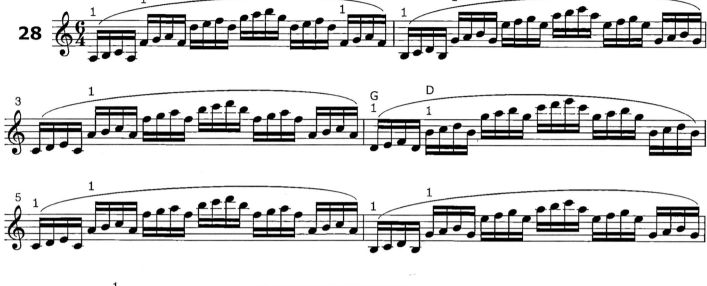

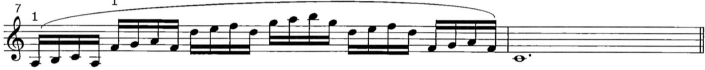

29

32

33

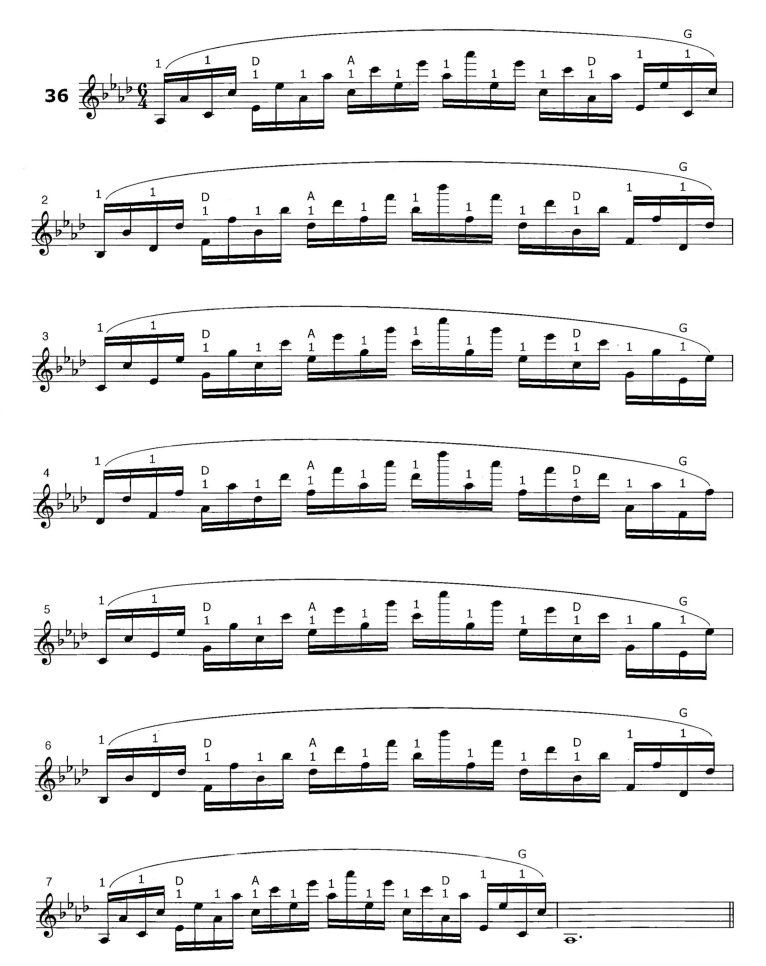

CHARLES CASTLEMAN is known internationally for solo performances with orchestras in Moscow, Brussels and Shanghai, masterclasses in London, Brisbane, Auckland, Vienna, Kiev, Seoul and Tokyo, and tours with the String Trio of New York and the Raphael Trio. Featured at the Australian, Budapest, Fuefukigawa, Marlboro and Vienna Festivals, his virtuoso music of Sarasate and Ysaye is available on *Music and Arts,* Gershwin and Antheil on *Musicmasters,* and the Amram Concerto on *Newport Classic.* Professor at the Eastman School of Music, he is the founder and director of The Quartet Program, a summer solo and chamber workshop praised by Yo-Yo Ma as "the best program of its kind . . . a training ground in lifemanship." His students have won prizes in the Szeryng Concours and at the Brussels, Munich, Leventritt and Naumberg competitions, are in 30 professionally active chamber groups, and are first desk players in the Philadelphia, St. Louis, Cincinnati, Milwaukee, Minnesota, Atlanta, Rochester, San Antonio, Los Angeles Chamber, and Tonhalle (Zurich) Orchestras. Mr. Castleman earned degrees from Harvard University, the Curtis Institute, and the University of Pennsylvania. His teachers were Emanuel Ondrícek (who was himself a student of Sevcik and Ysaÿe) and Ivan Galamian, and his most influential coaches were David Oistrakh, Henryk Szeryng and Josef Gingold. He plays the "Marquis de Champeaux" Stradivarius dating from 1708, and chooses from fifty fine bows.

ALLYSON DAWKINS is Principal Violist of the San Antonio Symphony. She is on the faculty of the University of Texas at San Antonio and is highly sought after and widely respected as a private teacher. She has performed at the Aspen Music Festival, Colorado Music Festival, Grand Teton Music Festival, Victoria Bach Festival, Peninsula Music Festival and Sunriver Music Festival. Ms. Dawkins received a Bachelor of Fine Arts degree from the State University of New York at Purchase, and a Master of Music degree and Performer's Certificate from the Eastman School of Music, where she was a student of Heidi Castleman.

The author wishes to thank Heidi Castleman, Professor of Viola at the Juilliard School of Music, for her continual guidance in playing and teaching the viola. She would also like to thank Mark Rogers, Director of Publications at Southern Music Company, for his help and patience in shepherding this project through to its completion.

Selected Violin Publications

METHODS

CROFT, DOROTHY

B195   **Violin Theory for Beginners, Bk. 1**   HL3770282

B196   **Violin Theory for Beginners, Bk. 2**   HL3770283

The 2nd book in a series developed by master string teacher Dorothy Croft to enhance the teaching of music theory in relation to the violin. A practical approach to teaching.

B522   **Violin Theory, Book One (Second Edition)**   HL3770867

Developed by master string teacher Dorothy Croft to enhance the teaching of music theory in relation to the violin. A practical approach to teaching.

HEIFETZ, JASCHA

Granat, Endre

S510010   **The Heifetz Scale Book (Softcover Edition)**   HL172780

For the first time ever, the new HEIFETZ SCALE BOOK presents all the great master violinist Jascha Heifetz' scale routines that were developed over his long career, but never written down! This edition by Heifetz protégé and world-class violinist Endre Granat is a self-contained master class for a lifetime of study in virtuoso technique.

The method is systematically presented in twelve units, one for each note in the chromatic scale. Contents include: two and four octave major, melodic and harmonic minor scales and arpeggios ● whole tone and chromatic scales ● double stop scales in all practical intervals ● trill studies ● scales with single and double harmonics ● left hand pizzicato

ONDRICEK, EMANUEL

Castleman, Charles/ Dawkins, Allyson

B568   **Superior Finger Exercises**   HL3770913

Emanuel Ondricek (1880 - 1958) was a phenomenal violin pedagogue in the early 20th century, whose students were praised for the musical fervor and remarkable left-hand facility. Filled with his collected exercises, the purpose of this book is to facilitate the learning of scales and arpeggios through a combination of visual and physical memory of the fingerboard.

SCHRADIECK, HENRY

Foltyn, Jaroslav

S510007   **School of Violin Technique, Book 1**   HL42650

This is the first new American edition in over a century. The fingerings by eminent Czech violinist and teacher, Jaroslav Foltyn, a master of teaching violin left hand technique, solve many technical issues that have existed for decades.

SEVCIK, OTAKAR

Granat, Endre/ Shipps, Stephen

S510008   **The Essential Sevcik**   HL119239

The Essential Sevcik is a compendium of the finest, most time-saving learning material by Otakar Sevcik ever assembled in a single volume. It is indispensable for building a thorough, virtuoso technique and an important part of the daily practice regimen for the accomplished artist. These exercises are to be practiced with total concentration and attention to the smallest detail. The clear and straight forward organization of this volume will facilitate finding the most suitable practice material for every violinist.

WOHLFAHRT, FRANZ

Wen, Eric

S510005   **60 Etudes for Violin, Op. 45, Bk. 1**   HL42303

Former Strad Magazine Editor-in-Chief, Eric Wen re-examines these classics with consideration for today's violinist with the first new, modern edition in almost one hundred years--meticulously re-engraved and attractively designed for years of use.

S510006   **60 Etudes for Violin, Op. 45, Bk. 2**   HL42391

With the first new edition in nearly 100 years, former Strad editor Eric Wen provides a 21st Century view of these classics. Book 2 includes modern fingerings as an alternative to the traditional, utilizing extensions, contractions, and half positions.

Exclusively distributed by  HAL•LEONARD® CORPORATION

Questions/ comments? info@laurenkeisermusic.com